The Highlands and Islands
Colouring Book

First published 2016
Reprinted 2019

The History Press
The Mill, Brimscombe Port
Stroud, Gloucestershire, GL5 2QG
www.thehistorypress.co.uk

Text © The History Press, 2016
Illustrations by Martin Latham © The History Press, 2016

British Library Cataloguing in Publication Data.
A catalogue record for this book is available from the British Library.

ISBN 978 0 7509 6801 0

Cover colouring by Lucy Hester.
Typesetting and origination by The History Press
Printed and bound by Imak, Turkey

THE HIGHLANDS AND ISLANDS

COLOURING BOOK

PAST AND PRESENT

Take some time out of your busy life to relax and unwind with this feel-good colouring book designed for everyone who loves the Highlands and Islands of Scotland.

Absorb yourself in the simple action of colouring in the scenes and settings from around Scotland, past and present. From majestic mountains to picturesque lochs, you are sure to find some of your favourite locations waiting to be transformed with a splash of colour. Bring these scenes alive as you de-stress with this inspiring and calming colouring book.

There are no rules – choose any page and any choice of colouring pens or pencils you like to create your own unique, colourful and creative illustrations.

Dunrobin Castle, Sutherland ▸

Castle Leod, Strathpeffer ▶

Cawdor Castle, Nairn ▸

Ring of Brodgar, a Neolithic henge
and stone circle in Orkney ▸

The recreated 1930s sitting room of Aultlarie tin cottage
at the Highland Folk Museum, Newtonmore ▶

Dolphins in the Moray Firth ▶

The ruins of Elgin Cathedral ▶

Fishing boats in Mallaig harbour, 1977 ▸

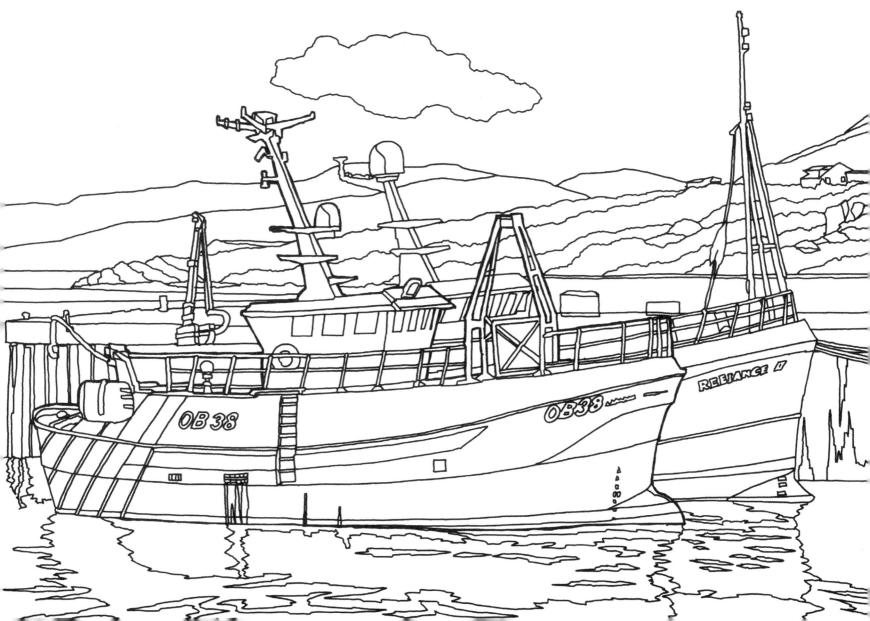

Fortrose Cathedral ▶

Dunnet Head, the most northerly
point of mainland Britain ▸

Skara Brae is a Neolithic settlement located in Orkney ▸

The ruin of Spynie Palace, Moray Firth ▶

Old Bridge, Sligachan, Isle of Skye ▶

St Andrew's Cathedral, Inverness ▶

St Magnus Cathedral, Orkney ▸

Strathspey Steam Railway ▸

Ullapool Beach ▶

Enjoying the view from Ben Nevis,
the highest mountain in the British Isles ▸

The Croft House Museum is a mid–nineteenth–century
Shetland croft, which was inhabited until the late 1960s ▸

Bow and Fiddle Rock, Portknockie ▶

The Caledonian Canal connects the Scottish east coast at
Inverness with the west coast at Corpach near Fort William ▸

Camels at the Highland Wildlife Park, near Kingussie ▶

Dunvegan Castle, Isle of Skye ▶

Eilean Donan Castle, Kyle of Lochalsh ▸

The majestic mountains of Glencoe ▶

Glenfinnan Viaduct on the West Highland Line ▶

Iona Abbey, Isle of Iona ▸

The Old Man of Storr, a rocky pinnacle on the Isle of Skye ▶

Alpacas at Black Isle Wildlife Park, North Kessock ▶

Tobermory, Isle of Mull ▸

Stunning scenery on the Isle of Harris ▸

Shetland ponies ▶

The ruins of Urquhart Castle sit
on the banks of Loch Ness ▸

Whaligoe Steps: 365 steps that descend to
what was once a landing place for fishing boats ▸

Highland cattle have long horns and long wavy coats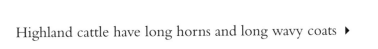

The ruins of the sixteenth-century
Ardvreck Castle, on the banks of Loch Assynt ▸

The ruins of Beauly Priory, founded *c.*1230 ▸

The Memorial Cairn is the largest
monument on Culloden Battlefield ▸

THE BATTLE
OF CULLODEN
16 of APRIL 1746

SCOTLAND PRINCE CHARLIE

Callanish Standing Stones, Isle of Lewis ▶

Jarlshof prehistoric and Norse settlement, Shetland ▸

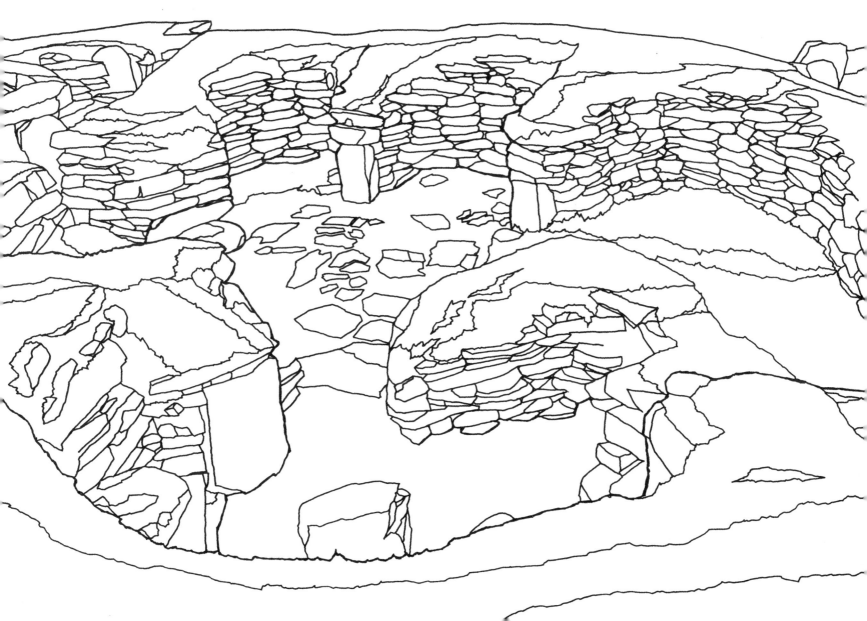

Portree, Isle of Skye ▶

Puffin on Handa Island ▶

Sangobeg Beach, Durness ▸

Inverness Victorian Market ▸

Dancing the Highland Fling ▶

Also from The History Press

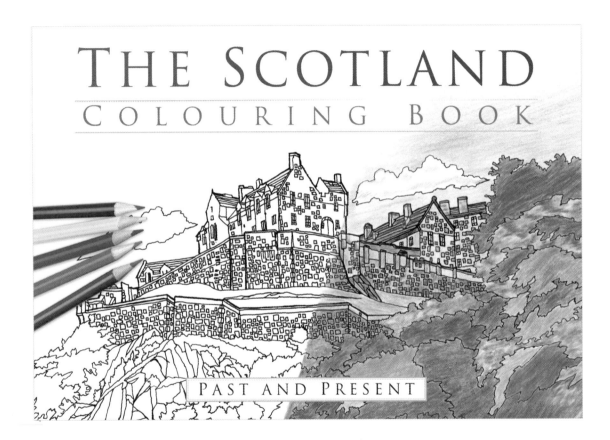

Find this colouring book and more at
www.thehistorypress.co.uk